D1413636

THIS BOOK
BELONGS TO

....

....

THE

Book of

LAVENDER

and

OLD LACE

An Inspiring Collection of Delightful
Projects and Pastimes from a Bygone Age

DEBORAH SCHNEEBELI-MORRELL

Photography by Heini Schneebeli

CHARTWELL
BOOKS, INC.

The Victorian Book of
Lavender and Old Lace

Designed and created by
THE BRIDGEWATER BOOK COMPANY LTD

Art Director: Peter Bridgewater
Designer: Jane Lanaway
Editor: Geraldine Christy
Managing Editor: Mandy Greenfield
Photography: Heini Schneebeli
Page make-up: Chris Lanaway

CHARTWELL BOOKS
A division of Book Sales, Inc.
114 Northfield Avenue
Edison, NJ 08837 USA

CLB 4086
© 1995 CLB Publishing
Godalming, Surrey

Color separation by HBM Print Ltd, Singapore
Printed and bound in Singapore by Tien Wah Press

ISBN 0-7858-0382-3

CONTENTS

INTRODUCTION

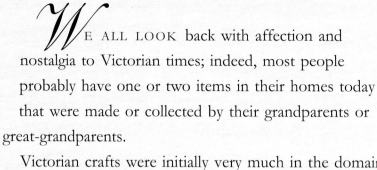

WE ALL LOOK back with affection and nostalgia to Victorian times; indeed, most people probably have one or two items in their homes today that were made or collected by their grandparents or great-grandparents.

Victorian crafts were initially very much in the domain of middle-class ladies. The industrial revolution had created a class of newly rich who were able to employ servants and had time on their hands. They developed quite extraordinary levels of creativity and technical ability across a wide range of media. Today, we marvel at their excellence.

Encouraged by the publication of fashionable ladies' magazines, their accomplishments covered such diverse crafts as stitchwork and embroidery, the painting of watercolours, the practising of penmanship, assembly of shell and seaweed pictures, a variety of flowercrafts and cut paperwork.

With the revival of interest in Victorian crafts, the projects in this book have been inspired by the spirit of those times.

Some are traditional and familiar, such as the pretty lace-edged pillow case and napkins on pages 18–19, simple to make, even for a novice needlewoman, with old lace used to its best effect. Or you can evoke lazy afternoon teas in the garden, by crocheting glittering beaded rows to antique lace or using crochet doilies to cover jugs of milk or cream, as on pages 38–9.

Découpage was a favourite craft in the nineteenth century, when a growing amount of decorative printed material became available for use. There are two lovely projects from which you can learn this wonderful craft. The hat box on pages 30–1, with its antique crackle glaze over Victorian fashion cuts, looks almost as if it might have been made 100 years ago. The tea tray on pages 32–3 is charming and, now that we can use polyurethane varnish to protect it from heat or wet, is suitably practical.

The Victorians loved their crafts to be pretty as well as practical, as is shown on pages 34–5 by the lavender-scented coat-hangers and fragrant sachets to slip amongst your clothes.

Other projects are more inventive but with a Victorian feel. Try making the lavender candles on pages 20–1, an unusual but surprisingly simple project.

Pot pourris and dried flower arrangements were a great favourite in Victorian homes. To show them at their best, display them in a stylish container, such as a china bowl that complements the pot pourri colours or, as on page 23, a pretty white creamware dish.

All the project ideas have been loosely based around the subjects of lavender, that fragrant summer shrub so easy to grow in your garden in all its many varieties, and old lace, which is still easy to find if you have not inherited some. Look in markets and antique shops, where you will find specialist stalls dealing in linen and old lace. Luckily, modern lace is often of a very high quality and indistinguishable from the old in style and pattern.

SLIPPER BAG

*V*ICTORIAN LADIES had servants who took great pride in keeping their mistress's clothes beautifully laundered. Items of clothing were packed with great care and skill in preparation for a journey. Shoes and slippers often decorated with bows, jewels, clasps, ribbons or laces were placed in their own bag so as not to snag or soil items of fine clothing in the suitcase, trunk or portmanteau.

MATERIALS

Blue damask 30 × 74 cm (12 × 30 in)
White and pale blue thread
1 m (3¼ ft) twisted satin cord with tassels attached
2 m (6½ ft) white ric rac
60 cm (24 in) white double-edged broderie anglaise
1 m (3¼ ft) white satin woven ribbon

1 Fold the damask halfway across the length, then tack and machine stitch up both sides.

2 Open the stitching on one side at the top. Turn 6 cm (2½ in) of fabric over the cord to make a hem, turning under 1.5 cm (½ in). Pin and tack.

3 Turn the bag right side out. Tack and then machine stitch ric rac along the hem line. Knot the two ends of the cord together to create a drawstring top.

WEDDING SLIPPERS

Queen Victoria's coronation slippers were of a ballet type, embroidered with rose buds and the royal arms in gold. They were lined in white satin reading 'All Hail Victoria' in a wreath of shamrock, thistle and roses.

4 From the inside, stitch the broderie anglaise one-third down onto the top of the bag. Turn the other two-thirds back to make a double 'frill', then iron.

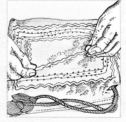

5 Lay ric rac and ribbon onto the front of the bag alternately as shown. First pin in place, then tack carefully and finally machine stitch.

6 If you wish the bag to have a soft, distressed, used look, dip the whole finished bag in tea for ten minutes, wash out, hang up and dry. Put the slippers in the bag, pull the cord and pack away.

LAVENDER POMANDERS

*T*HESE POMANDERS are simple and easy to make and are an inventive variation of the traditional clove-spiced oranges. Make them as modest presents for friends, hang them decoratively in airing cupboards, pile them loosely in a dainty basket or perhaps suspend them from differing lengths of pretty ribbon at a small window.

MATERIALS

7 cm (3 in) cotton (or polystyrene) balls
Pencil to hold ball
Mauve paint
Paintbrush for paint
PVA glue
Paintbrush for glue
Dried lavender flowers
1 m (3¼ ft) chiffon ribbon

1 *Pierce the cotton ball with a pencil to hold the ball firm. Paint the whole ball with mauve paint to match the colour of lavender flowers. Allow to dry.*

2 *Coat the ball with PVA glue and then roll it in a bowl of dried lavender flowers. Press into the flowers firmly until the ball is well covered. Allow to dry.*

3 *Tie the ribbon around the ball, dividing it into quarters, and glue it into the hole made by the pencil. Make a 'busy' bow with a collection of loops, adding one longer loop for hanging. Secure all into the glued hole at the top. Allow to dry before hanging.*

POT POURRI RECIPE

INGREDIENTS

1 crushed cinnamon stick
Half a teaspoon ground cloves
Half a teaspoon ground nutmeg
25 g (1 oz) orris root powder
3 drops lavender oil
2 drops bergamot oil
40 g (1½ oz) lavender
1 litre (1¾ pt) mixed blue mallow, rosemary, thyme, meadowsweet and lemon balm

1 *In a small box mix the cinnamon, cloves, nutmeg and orris root powder. Add the essential oils and rub between your fingers to ensure the oils are well mixed into the dry ingredients.*

2 *In a separate bowl place all the remaining dry ingredients. Mix together and then mix in the spices, orris powder fixative and essential oils.*

3 *Store in an airtight container for about six weeks to ensure the fragrance permeates the pot pourri and becomes mature. Transfer to a pretty bowl and decorate with dried flowers.*

LAMPSHADES

✦

OIL LAMPS and dim gas light were superseded in the 1880s by the incandescent gas mantle and shortly afterwards by the incandescent electric bulb. These bright lights inspired a new style for the Victorian parlour; gone were the days of soft pools of light in a richly cluttered room. A new taste for more simple design was emerging. These pretty lampshades are simple to make using ready-made shades.

SCALLOP-EDGED

MATERIALS

*Lampshade 16 cm (6½ in) high, with
bottom diameter 27 cm (11 in)*

Stiff white paper, A2 size

Tracing wheel

Hole punch

PVA paper glue

Double-sided sticky tape

1 Take the paper shade off the metal shade frame to use as a template. Lay the shade onto stiff white paper and extend the new shape beyond the bottom, making a scalloped edge by drawing around a cup rim.

2 With a tracing wheel, press firmly over a soft surface (e.g. an old magazine) through the paper around the scalloped edge and along the line of the old shade edge. With a hole punch, make a hole in the middle of each scallop.

3 Cut a smaller-scale scalloped edge to match at the top rim of the shade. Pierce with the hole punch and trace an embossed line to match the bottom rim.

4 Fix the top rim scallops to the shade with paper glue and when dry fix the shade around the frame, securing it at the join with invisible double-sided tape. It may be necessary to glue the paper shade to the metal rim at the top.

LACE AND RIBBON

Lace and ribbons were two essential items in a Victorian lady's sewing box and here they are used in a creative and really effective way. The 'lacy' ribbon is, in fact, a punched paper ribbon, commonly available in the nineteenth century.

MATERIALS

Lampshade 16 cm (6½ in) high, with bottom diameter 18 cm (7 in)

Pale mauve (lavender) paint

Wallpaper paste

1.5 m (5 ft) punched paper lacy ribbon

Craft knife

2 m (6½ ft) of 1.5 cm (½ in) wide blue and white gingham ribbon

2 With a craft knife cut 2 slits at the top and bottom of the shade all the way around between the lacy paper ribbon strips. The slits will be wider apart at the bottom than the top.

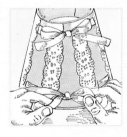

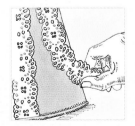

1 Paint the shade pale mauve, and allow to dry. Mix wallpaper paste and use it to paste 7 lengths of paper lacy ribbon vertically onto the shade.

3 Thread the ribbon behind the lace and through the slits between. Tie in little bows at the front of the lampshade.

PILLOWCASE AND NAPKINS

*D*OMESTIC ETIQUETTE was important in the Victorian household and so a variety of cutlery, china and table linen was kept for different culinary occasions. At tea the table was daintily set and tea-time napkins were often prettified with a lace trim.

PILLOWCASE

*T*his delightful child's pillowcase would make an ideal christening present. It is still possible to buy Victorian linen and lace in excellent condition although modern lace is often indistinguishable from old. This pillowcase is made from a combination of new and old material.

MATERIALS

Small linen pillowcase 48 × 32 cm (20 × 13 in)

Ornate lacy tray cloth 25 × 40 cm (10 × 16 in)

2.2 m (7 ft) of crochet lace 3.5 cm (1½ in) wide

Needle

White cotton

NAPKINS

MATERIALS

Pretty, old napkins 30 cm (12 in) square, with an embroidered posy in one corner if possible

1.5 m (5 ft) of soft lace 2.5 cm (1 in) wide

Small needle

White cotton

Sew the lace around the edge of the napkin with small neat stitches, taking care to gather the lace around the four corners so that it lies flat. To finish, the napkin may be starched and ironed.

1 Pin and tack the tray cloth onto the centre front of the pillowcase. Machine stitch in place, then remove tacking.

2 With small neat stitches, hand sew the lace around the edge of the pillowcase. Make two tucks at each corner to ensure the lace lies flat. Finish off neatly to disguise the join.

3 Starch and iron and fill with a fine down pillow.

*H*OW TO LAY A TABLE

Dinner, being the most important meal, is worthy of first place. Special attention must be paid to the table-linen which must always be perfectly clean, and free of creases. Serviettes may be folded in various shapes, the mitre being one of the most popular. This shape is only suitable for plain serviettes, and the bread-roll may be placed inside. Lace-edged napkins are usually folded in a fan shape and put in the tumblers.

Mrs Beeton's Household Management

LACE FIT FOR A QUEEN

Queen Victoria favoured Devonshire lace and in 1840 she ordered her wedding dress to be decorated with handmade Honiton lace. A Mistress Jane Bidney was given the task of gathering a team of one hundred of Devon's best lacemakers to work on the dress. Typical designs on Honiton lace were floral, including roses, thistles and shamrocks. Around 1880 rose blossoms and leaves with raised veins and edges were popular.

THE NAMING OF HONITON LACE

A Mrs Davey, who ran the lace shop in Honiton, received an order for a dress of Devonshire lace from Queen Charlotte, the wife of King George III. She called on many of the lacemakers of Devon to make the lace, using the long-lost art of mounting fine sprigs on a handmade net. The lacemakers delivered their work to her shop in Honiton, and so the Devon style of lacemaking got its name.

LAVENDER CANDLES

❧⚜❧

WAX CANDLES were expensive and only used in the grander houses or when visitors were expected. Tallow candles were chiefly for servants' use, although these too had to be used sparingly. Here is a lovely way to decorate wax candles with stems of dried lavender. Large candles have been used as they last a long time and provide a generous surface to work on.

MATERIALS

Dried stems of lavender

3 wax candles: 7 × 12 cm (3 × 5 in), 5 × 15 cm

(2 × 6 in) and 6 × 10 cm (2½ × 4 in)

Wax glue

Small double saucepan

Small paintbrush

Dipping can 8 × 20 cm (3 × 8 in)

1 kg (2.2 lb) paraffin wax beads

Deep saucepan

*Never choose your
women or your linen by candlelight.*

English Proverb

*My candle burns at both ends;
It will not last the night;
But oh my foes, and oh my friends –
It gives a lovely light.*

A Few Figs from Thistles
EDNA ST VINCENT MILLAY
1892–1950

1 Sort out some good straight stems of lavender and cut them approximately 1 cm (½ in) shorter than the candle they are to be stuck onto.

2 Melt a little wax glue over hot water in a small double saucepan. With the small paintbrush put spots of the melted glue onto the candle where the lavender will be placed. It dries quickly, so you may need to apply more glue while you work. Press the lavender onto the candle for a few seconds while it dries.

3 Continue sticking the lavender around the candle with this method, leaving between 1–1.5 cm (½–¾ in) between each stem and varying the heights.

4 Put the dipping can full of paraffin wax beads into a deep pan of very hot water. The wax will reduce as it melts. Do not cook the wax. It is ready for use as soon as it is melted.

5 Holding the candle by the wick, dip quickly in and out of the hot wax. You need only dip twice, as the more coats you use, the less colourful or visible the lavender becomes.

LAVENDER BUNDLES

N EWLY WASHED and ironed laundry was in the domain of the housekeeper; it was she who counted, checked and arranged it in the linen cupboard. Loose bundles of lavender were often placed between the layers of linen, from where they could impart their fresh clean scent. Here a generous bunch of lavender has been gathered together and tied with a rich purple wired ribbon. Such ribbons are widely available and their wire edges make it easy to tie, adjust and mould a sumptuous bow that will retain its shape.

HOW TO TIE
A WIRED BOW

1 Arrange the ribbon into two loops, and hold one in each hand.

And still she slept an azure lidded sleep
In blanched linen, smooth and lavendered
While he from forth the closet brought a heap
Of candied apple, quince, and plum, and gourd.

The Eve of St Agnes
JOHN KEATS

2 Fold the right loop over the left.

3 Fold the left loop over the right, under and through the hole, pull and tie into a bow.

DRIED FLOWERS

1 Fit the styrofoam into the bottom of the creamware bowl; cut to size if necessary.

$\mathcal{D}$URING THE long winter months, when fresh flowers were not available, garden flowers, which had been collected and dried during the summer in airy potting sheds, were arranged into beautiful floral displays. They were often protected under the characteristic glass domes so popular at the time. If you would like to dry your own flowers, collect loose bunches just before they are at their best. Bind the stems and hang up to dry in a warm airy place. The modest arrangement shown here is suitable for display on a windowsill, small shelf or mantelpiece.

2 With stems of approximately 5 cm (2 in), push the heads of the African marigolds into the styrofoam around the edge of the bowl.

*R*oses are red,
Lavender's blue,
If you will have me,
I will have you.

MATERIALS

Semi-spherical styrofoam
Creamware bowl
20 African marigold heads
Large bunch of double feverfew
Large bunch of dried lavender

3 Now make an inner circle of the double feverfew, making sure it is tightly packed against the marigolds.

4 Fill the large circular space in the middle of the display with lavender. It is easier to push in 4 or 5 stems together.

5 Pack the lavender in tightly until there is no space left. Check the arrangement carefully and make sure that all the flowers are even.

LACY-EDGED SHELVES

*T*HE VICTORIAN desire to prettify everything also extended to the humbler quarters of the house. The kitchen furniture, namely shelves and dressers, was often lined with patterned papers and sometimes this lining was extended into a lacy edge to the shelf, which it decoratively overhung.

MATERIALS

Large sheet of recycled paper (white)

Scissors

Pencil

Small jar lid as a template

Pinking shears

Hole punch

Small sheet pink paper

Brass upholstery tacks

Pin hammer

1 Cut a number of strips of the white paper 7 cm (3 in) wide. The number will depend on the length and number of shelves to be decorated.

2 Using a pencil, with the small round template touching one edge of the paper strip, draw a semi-circle. Keep drawing semi-circles along the strip.

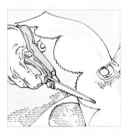

3 Cut around this line carefully with pinking shears.

*T*he labels on the glass storage jars have been made by photocopying and enlarging old cartouche designs, which are available in source books of copyright-free designs. These are then carefully cut out and stuck onto the jars. Try writing the names of the grains, cereals and pulses on the labels with Victorian copperplate writing.

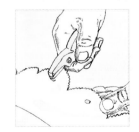

4 Punch a hole in the middle of each 'scallop' or semi-circle.

5 Cut 2 cm (³⁄₄ in)-wide strips of the pink paper and 'pink' both sides.

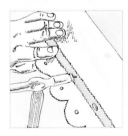

6 Lay the white paper straight side to match the top edge of the shelf, then lay the pink strip just below and fix firmly to the shelf edge with brass upholstery tacks.

*My son is my son till he gets
him a wife
But my daughter's my daughter all the
days of her life.*

English Proverb

VICTORIAN CARDS

THE VALENTINE ritual has its roots in pagan times, but the modern celebration commemorates St Valentine, a Roman priest who was executed for his faith in AD 270. He became the patron saint of lovers after his last act, a letter sent to his jailer's daughter signed 'from your Valentine'. Victorian ladies created their own individual Valentines in which they included poems and messages, often displaying elegant penmanship.

MATERIALS

Victorian facsimile scraps
Small scissors
Cream card
Paper glue
Pinking shears
Deep purple card
30 cm (12 in) of
glittery metallic ribbon
2.5 cm (1 in) wide

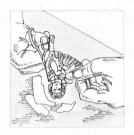

1 Choose and cut out a pretty Victorian scrap; a young girl holding a posy of garden flowers has been used here.

2 Stick the scrap centrally onto the cream card cut to 7 × 10 cm (3 × 4 in). Pink the edges of the card with pinking shears.

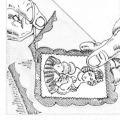

3 Stick the cream card onto a purple background card cut to 9 × 12 cm (3¹/₂ × 5 in). Cut the edges into scallops, marking the edge by using a coin as a template.

4 Make two ribbon-sized slits on the left of the card. Thread the ribbon through and tie into a pretty bow. Trim ribbon ends at an angle.

🎄 CHRISTMAS CARDS 🎄

Originally a German tradition, the sending of Christmas cards was introduced to England in the nineteenth century by Prince Albert, Queen Victoria's husband, and it soon became a well-established practice. There is a wide choice of Victorian scraps available with Christmas images. These are much richer in detail and colour than any contemporary designs. Here scraps have been used on a festive gold card background which has been mounted on a piece of maroon card. The design has been finished off with emblems from a gold doily and metallic gold braid.

Christmas is coming The goose is getting fat…

T U S S I E M U S S I E

*T*HE TUSSIE MUSSIE, a tightly bound posy of fragrant herbs and flowers, was commonly carried in the sixteenth century to disguise unpleasant smells and protect the bearer from the risk of disease. With the development of drainage and better hygiene in Victorian times, this practical use was abandoned and tussie mussies became popular as gifts. Make your own tussie mussies according to the seasons in your garden, as presents or commemorations of special occasions, or just to symbolize the enduring intimacy of friends.

A fresh tussie mussie will last about a week in water and may be dried afterwards by hanging it upside-down in a warm airy place.

MATERIALS

The herbs and flowers in this tussie mussie have been picked from a summer garden.

1 Start with a small posy for the centre and encircle it with a variety of contrasting herbs and flowers.

2 Bind the flower stems tightly with florist's wire as you go, adding little bunches of lavender throughout.

3 Gradually build up the layers, keeping the posy tight by binding the florist's wire around the newly added flowers.

4 Finish by encircling the tussie mussie with an outer ring of a large-leaved herb or, as in this case, small stems of curry herb. Bind to finish.

A tussie mussie should contain several sweet-smelling herbs. The name goes back to 1440 when it occurs in the first English–Latin dictionary: 'Tyte trust or tusmose of flowers or other herbs = olfactorium.' Tussie mussies are obviously similar to the highly scented nosegays carried by judges. In the Colonies, ladies would carry them to church on Sundays and in Victorian times they were sometimes used to send a message through the symbolism of flowers.

PIN CUSHION

NEEDLEWORK WAS an important aspect of a Victorian lady's list of accomplishments. The sewing box was common to all homes, containing pins and needles made of steel, which were expensive and rusted easily. Airtight ivory or bone needlecases became popular and in order to conserve their precious pins, women designed and fashioned the most exquisite pin cushions.

She will surely be undone, who wears a pin in her Bridal Gown.

English Proverb

MATERIALS

Half a metre (1½ ft) of woollen paisley

15 cm (6 in) polyester wadding

70 cm (28 in) pleated black ribbon-edged braid

1 m (3¼ ft) small-beaded braid

Black cotton

Steel pins

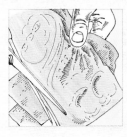

1 Cut the paisley fabric into pieces: 2 pieces 12 × 10 cm (5 × 4 in), 2 pieces 12 × 6 cm (5 × 2½ in) and 2 pieces 10 × 6 cm (4 × 2½ in).

2 Pin and tack together into a rectangular 'box' shape, leaving open one side.

3 Turn the right way out and stuff with polyester wadding until the cushion is quite firm. Sew up the side.

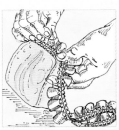

4 Sew black braid around the sides like a 'skirt'.

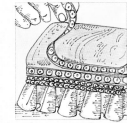

5 Sew two rows of the beaded braid around the perimeter of the cushion.

6 Make a flower pattern and border with steel pins, by pushing them firmly into the cushion.

DÉCOUPAGE HAT BOX

HATS WERE an essential part of every woman's wardrobe, from scullery maids to ladies of the highest rank. It was important that they were stored carefully in hat boxes to protect them from dust and sunlight.

Découpage was a favourite Victorian craft. Use this technique to make an authentic-looking hat box which, in 'the absence of any hats', could be a very useful storage box.

… it is not that artistic power has left the world, but that a more rapid life has developed itself in it, leaving no time for deliberate dainty decoration, or labours of love.

The Drawing Room and its Decorations
MRS ORRIN SMITH 1877

MATERIALS

Large circular box with lid (cardboard or plywood), 35 cm (14 in) in diameter, 18 cm (7 in) deep

Dull blue paint

Paintbrush for paint

Small scissors

Ladies' fashion cuts for découpage

Wallpaper paste

Paper lace

Crackle glaze (water-based) stages 1 and 2

Paintbrush for crackle glaze

Rag

Burnt umber oil paint

Polyurethane satin-finish varnish

1 Paint the box blue. Use two coats to ensure good cover.

2 With a small pair of scissors carefully cut out a selection of black and white ladies' fashion engravings.

3 Mix the wallpaper paste, and paste the cutouts onto the sides and lid of the box. Paste strips of vertical paper lace onto the side of the box between the fashion cuts. Paste the frilly-edged lace around the top, bottom and lid rim of the box. Allow to dry.

4 Paint stage 1 of the crackle glaze onto the box (following the manufacturer's instructions). Allow to dry. Paint stage 2 of the crackle glaze. Dry it quickly with a hair dryer and the cracks will soon appear.

5 With a rag, rub in the burnt umber paint to fill in the cracks. Wipe off excess paint with a clean rag, holding it as flat as possible so as not to pull the pigment out of the cracks. Allow to dry and varnish with two or three coats of polyurethane varnish to protect.

*Blond lace may be revived by
breathing upon it, and shaking and flapping it.
The use of the iron turns the lace yellow.*

Enquire Within
Upon Everything 1894

The cosy fire is bright and gay,
The merry kettle boils away
And hums a cheerful song.
I sing the saucer and the cup;
Pray, Mary, fill the tea-pot up,
And do not make it strong.

The Poets at Tea, 'Cowper'
BARRY PAIN 1864–1928

TEA TIME

*I*T WAS the footman's job to serve tea upstairs. For everyday purposes a tray was brought to the drawing room and tea was laid out on a small table. This lovely découpaged tea tray will give you great pleasure to use and is simple to make. It has been effectively antiqued to give it a Victorian look; black and white flower engravings have been used along with scrolls, both photocopied from source books of nineteenth-century botanical illustrations and decorative borders.

MATERIALS

Metal tray

Oil-based metal primer (if tray is unpainted)

Water-based lilac paint

Paintbrush for paint

Small pointed scissors

Prints of botanical illustrations and scrolls or other source material

Wallpaper paste

Crackle glaze stages 1 and 2

Burnt umber oil paint for antiquing

2 rags

Polyurethane satin-finish varnish

Paintbrush for varnish

Turpentine for cleaning varnish brush

> *A young girl who puts sugar in her tea after pouring the milk will surely stay a spinster.*
>
> E n g l i s h   P r o v e r b

1 Paint the tray with the metal primer. If it is already painted, after a light sanding apply two coats of lilac-coloured paint.

2 With the small scissors carefully cut out the botanical illustrations and scrolls.

3 Apply the paste to the tray and stick the prints down, easing out any trapped air bubbles. Apply the scrolls to the edges and centre.

4 Apply the crackle glaze, stages 1 and 2. The second coat may be dried with a hair dryer to encourage the glaze to crackle more quickly.

5 Rub burnt umber paint into the cracks with a small rag. Wipe off the excess with a clean rag.

6 Allow to dry and finish off with at least two coats of polyurethane varnish. For a really smooth finish lightly sand the penultimate coat.

LAVENDER LAUNDRY

A lavender bush growing near a clothes line can serve as a useful dryer for handkerchiefs, leaving them fresh and fragrant smelling. There is a Christian tale of how the lavender plant gained its scent. The new mother Mary left the clothes of the infant Jesus to dry on a lavender bush. When she picked up the clothes they had a beautiful, fresh smell. From then on, the lavender plant was always fragrant.

MUCH ATTENTION was paid to the care of the Victorian wardrobe. Dresses for special occasions were made of a great variety of exquisite materials and trimmings, and needed to be carefully stored and hung. The soft padding of this coat-hanger encloses a fragrant quantity of dried lavender flowers, the traditional fragrance for wardrobes. The little sachets made to match, with their fresh lavender scent, will help to keep the moths at bay.

LAVENDER
COAT-HANGERS

MATERIALS

2 wire coat-hangers

25 cm (10 in) each of grey and purple shot silk

25 cm (10 in) polyester wadding

2 handfuls of dried lavender flowers

Matching thread and needle

1 m (3¼ ft) lace for trimming the grey hanger

. 50 cm (20 in) lace for trimming the purple hanger

30 cm (12 in) each of silk checked ribbon and mauve silk ribbon

1 Lay the coat-hanger onto the silk and cut a double length, half as long again as the hanger, 9 cm (3½ in) wide.

2 Cut the wadding slightly longer than the hanger and wrap around. Before sewing it up loosely, fill with dried lavender.

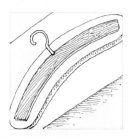 

3 With the hanger inside the silk, turn under a 1 cm (½ in) hem. Slot the lace between the seam, pin, then sew with running stitch, gathering the thread every 10 cm (4 in) .

4 Finish off neatly at the handle, then bind the handle with similar-coloured ribbon and tie with a wired bow.

LAVENDER
SACHETS

MATERIALS

Off-cuts of the same silk as used for the coat-hangers

1 m (3¼ ft) each of fine lace and broderie anglaise for the trim

Needle and thread

Lavender flowers

Ribbons in a faded colour to match the silk

 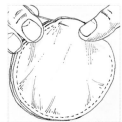

1 Cut silk into shape: square 10 × 10 cm (4 × 4 in) or circle 10 cm (4 in) in diameter.

2 With right sides together, enclosing the gathered lace or broderie anglaise into the seam, stitch with small stitches or machine the seam, leaving a 5 cm (2 in) opening.

3 Turn inside out, fill with lavender flowers and finish off the opening neatly. Tie a small bow and sew in place.

BOTTLES

HERBS AND flowers have been used over the centuries in the making of cosmetics and to this day they remain important ingredients in health and beauty preparations. Many of these recipes have been handed down from mother to daughter through all ages and cultures. Perfumed floral waters, lavender being a particular favourite of the Victorians, have refreshing astringent qualities, and when decanted into pretty glass bottles they become delightful accessories to grace a lady's dressing table.

LAVENDER WATER

INGREDIENTS

One cup lavender flowers and leaves

Airtight container

300 ml (½ pt) cider vinegar or white wine vinegar

A fine sieve

Jug

150 ml (¼ pt) rosewater

1 Put the lavender flowers and leaves into the airtight container and pour over the vinegar. Put the lid on and allow to infuse for about three days in a cool dark place; shake twice daily.

2 After three days, strain the lavender through a fine sieve into a jug.

3 Add the rosewater to the lavender infusion and stir to mix thoroughly.

4 Decant into pretty bottles and tie with wired silk bows for a really sumptuous effect.

ESSENTIAL OILS

Essential oils are pure, concentrated essences of plants which are prepared by distillation. This is a lengthy and laborious process that requires much knowledge and skill. Very large quantities of flowers are needed to produce very small quantities of oil. The housekeeper and still-room maid were party to this knowledge in the nineteenth century and used essential oils in the preparation of oils, tinctures and ointments. Nowadays it is more practical to buy them, as they are so readily available. A few drops in a bath creates a wonderful fragrance and is therapeutic.

His Aunt Jobiska made him drink,
Lavender water tinged with pink,
For she said, The World in general knows
There's nothing so good for a Pobble's toes!

The Pobble who has no Toes
EDWARD LEAR 1812–88

LAVENDER-SCENTED MASSAGE OIL

Simply add eight drops of lavender essential oil to a proprietary blend of unscented massage oil. Mix two oils together for a richer scent. Try rose and lavender, and violet and jasmine.

LACY BEAD COVERS

*I*N THE summer months, when tea was regularly taken in the garden on fine days, perhaps as a refreshing break during a game of croquet or tennis, pretty lacy beaded crochet covers were used to keep dust and small insects from falling into jugs of home-made cordial, milk or cream, or bowls of sugar. They were also used to cover basins of food in the pantry.

*T*he pretty beaded covers shown here have been made by using a crocheted edge to attach a row of glittering coloured glass beads to antique doilies. The number of beads used depends on the circumference of your doily. For the large beaded cover (diameter 22 cm/9 in) with the pink and clear glass beads, you will need 24 pink and 24 clear beads. For the smaller cover (diameter 15 cm/6 in) you will need 32 blue beads, alternately opaque and clear.

MATERIALS

Selection of coloured glass beads with large central holes

White crochet cotton, approximately the same gauge as the existing doily

Number 12 crochet hook

Antique crocheted doilies

*O*f course, your ladyship knows that such lace must never be starched or ironed. Some people wash it in sugar and water, and some in coffee, to make it the right yellow colour; but I myself have a very good receipt for washing it in milk, which stiffens it enough, and gives it a very good creamy colour.

Cranford
MRS GASKELL
1810–65

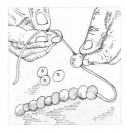

1 Thread the correct number of beads onto the crochet cotton.

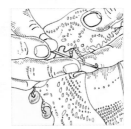

2 Crochet loops of twelve chains, slipping a bead onto the chain before joining it to the edge of the doily.

3 Continue with these twelve chain loops around the circumference until all the beads are threaded on. Finish off neatly.

LACY PICTURE FRAME

*T*HERE WERE always many images to frame in the Victorian household. And with the invention of photography and the new advances in the printing industry, all families could now afford to hang a whole range of family portraits. This simple frame has been decoratively enhanced by carefully cutting and pasting a lacy paper doily onto it.

MATERIALS

Picture frame 26 × 32 cm (10 × 13 in) with front border 7 cm (3 in) wide

This frame has 1.5 cm ($\frac{1}{2}$ in) raised bands on the inside and outside edge of the front

Brick-red paint

Paintbrush

Small sharp scissors

Assortment of square and rectangular doilies

Wallpaper paste and brush

White paper

Pinking shears

Polyurethane varnish

Brush for varnish

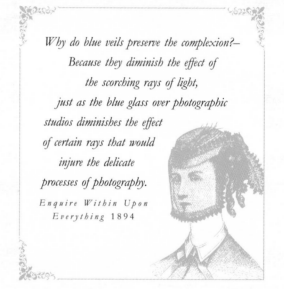

Why do blue veils preserve the complexion?—
Because they diminish the effect of
the scorching rays of light,
just as the blue glass over photographic
studios diminishes the effect
of certain rays that would
injure the delicate
processes of photography.

Enquire Within Upon
Everything 1894

1 Paint the frame with two coats of brick-red paint.

2 Cut out sections of a paper doily so that they fit around the frame neatly.

3 Arrange the pieces of doily around the frame. Paste the frame and stick the doily in place. Smooth out any air bubbles with your fingers.

4 Cut strips of white paper on both sides with the pinking shears and paste onto the rims of the frame.

5 Finally, varnish with two or three coats of polyurethane varnish. Lightly sand the penultimate coat to achieve a smooth finish.

*One picture is worth
a thousand words.*

Chinese Proverb

CORNUCOPIAS

*A*LL MANNER of delicious and appealing desserts, sweetmeats, crystallized fruits and bonbons were served with the coffee after an excellent meal. These little gold paper cornucopias are lined with pretty patterned paper and trimmed with paper lace and ribbons to make them into mouth-watering offerings.

MATERIALS

Template (see page 45 for an example which can be reduced or enlarged)

Sheet of gold card

Sharp pencil

Scissors, large and small

Printed patterned paper (gift wrap) for lining

Wallpaper paste

Double-sided tape

Scraps of white paper for trimming

Pinking shears

Hole punch

Pink paper lace

FRINGES AND BRAIDS

*M*ake a variety of cornucopias and vary the decorative edging. Try using fringes or braids. A folded length of paper that has been 'pinked' vertically into a fringe is particularly effective. Make a special flourish with a glittery ribbon and bow to finish.

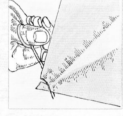

1 Draw around the template with a sharp pencil. Be careful not to scratch the gold card. Cut out with the larger scissors. Use the small scissors to cut the point as shown.

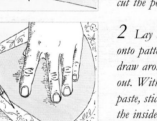

2 Lay the template onto patterned paper, draw around it and cut out. With the wallpaper paste, stick this paper onto the inside of the gold card. Allow to dry thoroughly.

3 Bend the card gently around and lay a strip of double-sided tape on one side of the cone shape. Bring the other side around and evenly over the tape. Press to stick firmly.

4 Trim back the opening on the top so that the final contents are more easily revealed.

5 *Using a small round template (e.g. a film canister) draw a scalloped edge on a white paper strip. Cut out with pinking shears to create a decorative edge. Punch holes in the centre of the scallops and then stick around the opening with double-sided tape, lining up the join with the seam on the back of the cone.*

6 *Finish off by sticking on pink paper lace in the same way. Leave it partly protruding over the edge and fold and stick back inside the cone. This makes a neat edge and disguises the cut rim of the cone.*

INDEX

ACKNOWLEDGEMENTS

The author would like to give
very special thanks to Heini
Schneebeli for his care and attention to
detail in taking the really lovely photographs in
this book. And to all my good friends who have
happily lent me beautiful objects from their own homes:
Raynes Minns, Naomi Gornick, Alan Stewart and Anthea
Sieveking, my mother Dulcie Beilin Morel, Sarah Fitzgerald and Sophie
Hedworth. Particular thanks to Gloria Nichol for all her supportive advice
during the making of this book and to Graham Day for his creative help; to
Catherine Buckley for the loan of the blue satin slippers on page 13; to Lakeland Plastics
Ltd, Alexandra Buildings, Windermere, Cumbria, LA23 1BQ for supplying paper doilies; and to
Mamelok Press Ltd, Bury St Edmunds, IP32 6NJ, for supplying the Victorian scraps used on pages 26
and 27. The cartouche designs on pages 24 and 25, and engravings on pages 32 and 33, were photocopied
from copyright-free source books published by Dover Publications.
Very special thanks to my two children, Hannah and Raphael, and to Teo Spurring, who have been so patient,
understanding and supportive during the production of this book. Special thanks also to Anna Bentinck for
her invaluable help with finding the original Victorian material.

Cornucopia template (see page 42) – this can be enlarged or reduced as desired